SUSAN B. ANTHONY

EQUAL RIGHTS LEADERS

Don McLeese

Rourke
Publishing LLC
Vero Beach, Florida 32964

www.rourkepublishing.com

PHOTO CREDITS:
All photos courtesy of Susan B. Anthony House, Rochester, NY

Cover Photo: *Susan B. Anthony, circa 1858, Rochester, NY*

EDITOR: Frank Sloan

COVER DESIGN: Nicola Stratford

Library of Congress Cataloging-in-Publication Data

McLeese, Don.
  Susan B. Anthony / Don McLeese.
     p. cm. — (Equal rights leaders)
Includes bibliographical references and index.
Contents: Equal rights for all — Quaker girl — A woman's place — Teaching and learning — Many causes — Women's rights movement — Under arrest — A national hero — Her memory lives on.
  ISBN 1-58952-284-2 (Hardcover)
  1. Anthony, Susan B. (Susan Brownell), 1820-1906—Juvenile literature.
2. Feminists—United States—Biography—Juvenile literature. 3.
Suffragists—United States—Biography—Juvenile literature. [1. Anthony,
Susan B. (Susan Brownell), 1820-1906. 2. Suffragists. 3. Women--Biography.] I.
Title.

  HQ1413.A55 M388 2002
  324.6'23'092--dc21   2002002041

Printed in the USA

MP/W

TABLE OF CONTENTS

Equal Rights for All   5
Quaker Girl   6
A Woman's Place   9
Teaching and Learning   11
Many Causes   12
Women's Rights Movement   14
Under Arrest   17
A National Hero   18
Her Memory Lives On   21
Important Dates to Remember   22
Glossary   23
Index   24
Further Reading/Websites To Visit   24

Equal Rights for All

Susan B. Anthony worked hard for **equal rights** for all Americans. She believed that women should be treated the same as men. She also believed that **slavery** should be outlawed. Before the **Civil War**, many **African Americans** were owned by white people. They were known as slaves and they had to work without being paid. Susan knew this was wrong.

Susan B. Anthony (left) and biographer Ida Husted Harper, 1898

Quaker Girl

Susan Brownell Anthony was born on February 15, 1820. Her father, Daniel, owned a cotton mill. Her mother was named Lucy. The family believed in the **Quaker** religion. Quakers said that men and women were equal, and that slavery and war were evil. Susan learned a lot from her religion.

Susan's birthplace, Adams, Massachusetts

A Woman's Place

When Susan was growing up, women weren't allowed to vote or own property. Many people felt that a woman's place was in the home. Women were expected to cook and clean, keep house, and raise the children while men went to work. Those few women who took jobs outside the house were paid much less than men.

Susan as a young reformer

Teaching and Learning

Susan finished school when she was 17 and started teaching. This is one of the few jobs women were allowed to hold. After the family moved to Rochester, New York, in 1845, Susan continued to work as a teacher. The job paid her only $2.00 a week. She learned that men doing the same job were paid four or five times more.

Susan as a teacher

Many Causes

Susan stayed busy with many causes. She worked to end slavery and to outlaw **liquor**, because Quakers were against both. When she tried to speak at rallies, she was told that women should "listen and learn," while the men did the talking. She knew that if women had the same rights as men, she could help society in other ways.

Susan's new home after moving to Rochester, New York

Women's Rights Movement

   While working against slavery, Susan met Elizabeth Cady Stanton in 1851. For the rest of the century, Susan and Elizabeth were the two strongest leaders for women's rights. They started the American Equal Rights Association. They also published a newspaper. Susan and Elizabeth said they wanted "justice for all," women and men, black and white.

Susan and Elizabeth Cady Stanton

Under Arrest

Women weren't allowed to vote, and Susan was arrested when she went to vote. In 1873, a New York judge said she had to pay a fine of $100 for trying to vote. Susan refused, but she wasn't sent to jail. She said in a speech that the rights of Americans are for "we, the people, not we, the white male citizens."

"Failure Is Impossible" was Susan's slogan.

A National Hero

In the early 1900s, Susan met with President Theodore Roosevelt about letting women vote. In Washington, D.C., she gave a speech where she said, "Failure is impossible." She died on March 13, 1906. In 1920, Congress passed the 19th **Amendment** to the Constitution. It is known as the "Susan B. Anthony Amendment" because it gave women the right to vote.

Susan in the 1890s

Her Memory Lives On

In 1979, the United States issued a silver dollar coin with a picture of Susan B. Anthony on it. It was called the Susan B. Anthony dollar.

The Susan B. Anthony House, where she lived in Rochester, N.Y., is open as a museum. It is a National Historic Landmark. People from all over the country come to honor the woman who did so much for equal rights.

*A Susan B. Anthony
silver dollar necklace*

Important Dates to Remember

1820	Susan B. Anthony is born
1845	Family moves to Rochester, New York
1851	Susan B. Anthony meets Elizabeth Cady Stanton
1906	Susan B. Anthony dies

GLOSSARY

African Americans (aff RIH kun uh MARE ih kuns) — black people, Americans whose early relatives came from Africa

Amendment (uh MEND ment) — an addition that changes the Constitution of the United States

Civil War (SIV ul WAR) — a war between the North and South in the United States, from 1861-65; the North won and made slavery illegal

equal rights (EE kwil RITES) — the same rights for everyone in society

liquor (LICK ur) — a drink with alcohol

Quaker (KWAY kur) — member of a Christian religion that strongly believes in peace and equal rights, also known as the Society of Friends

slavery (SLAY vur ee) — when one person owns other people and makes them work without pay

INDEX

19th Amendment   18
American Equal Rights
   Association   14
equal rights   14
father and mother   6
Roosevelt, President Theodore
   18
Stanton, Elizabeth Cady   14
Susan B. Anthony dollar   21
Susan B. Anthony House   22
teacher   11
women's rights   14

Further Reading

Raatma, Lucia. *Susan B. Anthony.* Compass Point Books, 2001.
Rustad, Martha E. *Susan B. Anthony*. Capstone Press, 2001.

Websites To Visit

http://www.susanbanthonyhouse.org
http://www.rochester.edu/SBA/

About The Author

Don McLeese is an award-winning journalist whose work has appeared in many newspapers and magazines. He is a frequent contributor to the World Book Encyclopedia. He and his wife, Maria, have two daughters and live in West Des Moines, Iowa.

UPHAMS CORNER

BAKER & TAYLOR